Relatives of Dinosaurs

Robin Birch

CHELSEA
CLUBHOUSE

An Imprint of Chelsea House Publishers

This edition published in 2009 in the United States of America by Chelsea Clubhouse, an imprint of Chelsea House Publishers.

Chelsea Clubhouse
An imprint of Chelsea House Publishers
132 West 31st Street
New York, NY 10001

Chelsea Clubhouse books are available at special discounts when purchased in bulk quantities for businesses, associations, institutions, or sales promotions. Please call our Special Sales Department in New York at (212) 967-8800 or (800) 322-8755.

You can find Chelsea Clubhouse on the World Wide Web at: http://www.chelseahouse.com

First published in 2002 by
MACMILLAN EDUCATION AUSTRALIA PTY LTD
15–19 Claremont Street, South Yarra, 3141

Visit our Web site at www.macmillan.com.au or go directly to www.macmillanlibrary.com.au

Associated companies and representatives throughout the world.

Copyright © Robin Birch 2009; 2002

Library of Congress Cataloging-in-Publication Data
Birch, Robin.
   Relatives of dinosaurs / by Robin Birch.
   v. cm. — (Dinosaur world)
   Includes index.
   Contents: Dinosaurs — Reptiles — Pliosaurs — Plesiosaurs — Pterosaurs — A giant crocodile — A giant turtle — Names and their meanings.
   ISBN 978-1-60413-408-7
   1. Animals, Fossil—Juvenile literature. [1. Prehistoric animals.] I. Title. II. Series.
   QE861.5 .B57 2009
   566—dc21
                                                        2008000842

Edited by Angelique Campbell-Muir
Illustrations by Nina Sanadze
Page layout by Nina Sanadze

Printed in the United States of America

Acknowledgements
Department of Library Services, American Museum of Natural History (neg. no. 6744), p. 16; Auscape/ Francois Gohier, pp. 5, 12; The Field Museum (neg. no. GEO85818c), p. 7 (bottom); © The Natural History Museum, London, pp. 20, 25, 28; Royal Tyrrell Museum of Palaeontology/Alberta Community Development, p. 7 (top); Southern Images/Silkstone, p. 8.

While every care has been taken to trace and acknowledge copyright, the publisher tenders their apologies for any accidental infringement where copyright has proved untraceable.

Contents

Glossary words
When a word is printed in **bold**, you can look up its meaning in the Glossary on page 31.

Dinosaurs

Dinosaurs lived millions of years ago. Some dinosaurs ate animals and others ate plants.

There were many different kinds of dinosaurs.

Some dinosaurs were big and some were small.

Dinosaurs were all different sizes.

Reptiles

Reptiles are **cold-blooded** animals. They breathe air through their lungs, lay eggs, and have **scales** on their skin. Dinosaurs were reptiles.

scale

All reptiles have scales on their skin.

Lizards and snakes are reptiles that live on Earth today.

Lizard

Snake

Dinosaurs were reptiles that walked on land. They held their legs underneath their bodies, not out to the side as lizards do. There were no swimming or flying dinosaurs.

lizard   dinosaur

Lizards and dinosaurs held their legs differently.

Many swimming and flying reptiles did live in the time of the dinosaurs. They were relatives of dinosaurs.

These reptiles lived at the same time as the dinosaurs.

Pliosaurs

(PLEE-o-sawrs)

Pliosaurs were huge reptiles that lived in seas, lakes, and rivers. These swimmers ate other reptiles as well as fish and **shellfish**.

sharp teeth

long head

Pliosaurs had long heads. Long, sharp teeth filled their mouths. Their necks were short. They were very fierce **predators** and could catch any animal that lived in the water.

strong flipper

Pliosaurs were huge dinosaurs that lived underwater.

Pliosaurs had a tail and four big, strong flippers.
They moved their flippers up and down to swim.
Pliosaurs could swim very fast to catch their **prey**.

Pliosaurs fed on prey that lived underwater.

Scientists have dug up pliosaur bones to study.
These **fossils** show us how pliosaurs looked.

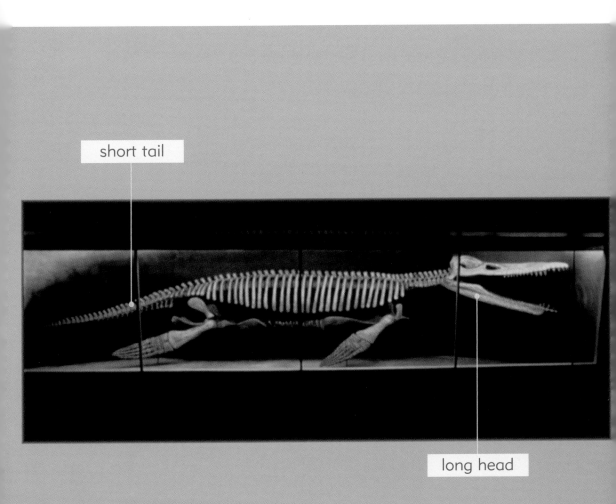

short tail

long head

This Pliosaur skeleton shows us what they looked like.

Plesiosaurs

(PLES-ee-oh-sawrs)

Plesiosaurs were swimming reptiles that ate fish. They had small heads and sharp teeth. Their necks were very long.

very long neck

14

Plesiosaurs had wide bodies, like turtles without shells. They had four flippers and a tail.

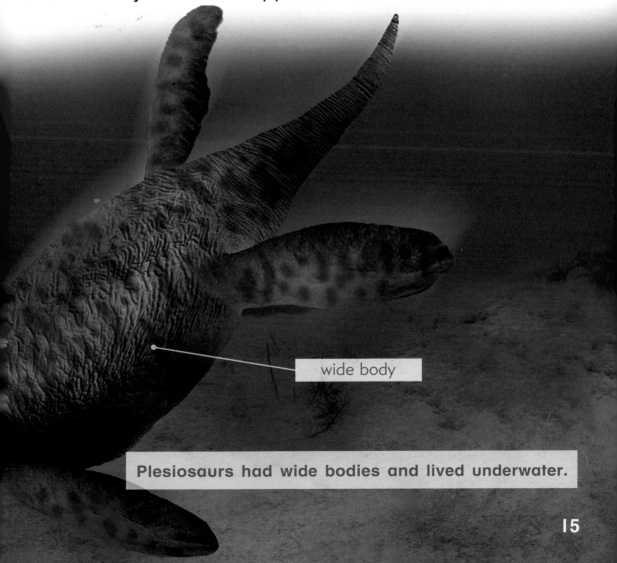

wide body

Plesiosaurs had wide bodies and lived underwater.

Plesiosaurs lived in seas, lakes, and rivers. Like other swimming reptiles, plesiosaurs came to the surface to breathe air.

Plesiosaurs lived underwater but swam to the surface to breathe

Plesiosaurs could probably move on land by dragging themselves with their flippers, as turtles that live in water do today. They most likely laid eggs in nests in beach sand.

Turtles come onto land to lay their eggs, just as Plesiosaurs once did.

Pterosaurs

(TAIR-oh-sawrs)

Pterosaurs were flying reptiles. There were many different kinds of pterosaurs.

no teeth

Pteranodon (tuh-RAN-uh-don) was one of the biggest pterosaurs. Its **wingspan** was about 25 feet (7.5 meters). Pteranodon had no teeth. It probably used its beak to scoop up fish from the sea.

long wing

This Pteranodon was one of the largest Pterosaurs.

The small pterosaur Rhamphorhynchus (RAM-for-INK-uhs) had sharp teeth to spear fish from the sea. It had a diamond-shaped flap of skin on its tail to keep it steady as it flew. Including its tail, Rhamphorhynchus was about 3 feet (1 meter) long. It had a wingspan of about 3 feet (1 meter).

Rhamphorhynchus used its sharp teeth to spear fish.

Pterosaurs had good eyesight and were excellent hunters. They dived into the sea to catch fish as many sea birds do today.

Sea birds today dive for fish in the same way that Pterosaurs did.

A Giant Crocodile

Many types of crocodiles lived at the same time as the dinosaurs. They were very much like the crocodiles that live today.

strong teeth

The biggest known crocodile was Deinosuchus (DIE-noh-SOOK-uhs). It was a giant crocodile that measured 50 feet (15 meters) long. It lived in **swamps**, where it caught fish and small reptiles to eat.

strong tail

Deinosuchus was a giant crocodile that looked a lot like the crocodiles that live today.

Deinosuchus probably laid its eggs in nests, as crocodiles do today.

Crocodiles lay their eggs in a nest.

Crocodiles today carry their young in their mouths. Deinosuchus probably carried its young in the same way.

Crocodiles carry their young in their mouths.

A Giant Turtle

Several kinds of turtles lived at the same time as the dinosaurs. One was a giant sea turtle called Archelon (ARK-uh-lahn).

flipper

Archelon was about 13 feet (4 meters) long. It had a wide, flat shell and a short tail. It moved its four paddle-shaped flippers up and down to swim in the sea.

wide shell

Archelon was a giant turtle that lived in the sea.

Archelon had a narrow head with a beak that curved downward. It probably ate **jellyfish** as sea turtles do today.

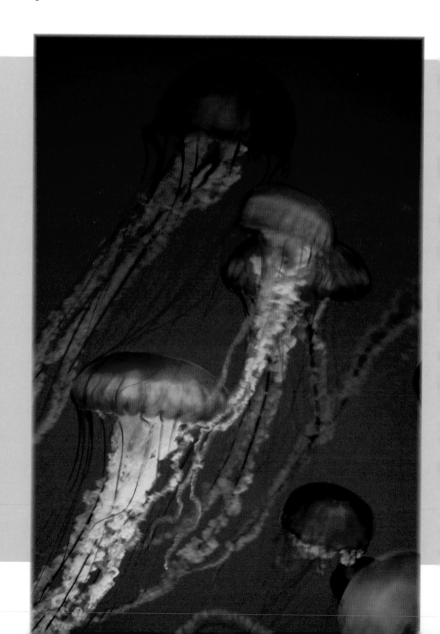

Turtles today eat jellyfish like these.

Female Archelons laid their eggs in nests on sandy beaches. Newly hatched Archelons probably ran together to the sea in the same way that young sea turtles do today.

Young sea turtles run to the sea after they are hatched.

Names and Their Meanings

"Dinosaur" means "terrible lizard."

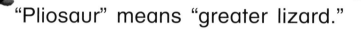

"Pliosaur" means "greater lizard."

"Plesiosaur" means "near lizard"; plesiosaurs were given this name because they were related to the dinosaurs.

"Pterosaur" means "winged lizard."

"Pteranodon" means "winged and toothless."

"Rhamphorhynchus" means "beak nose."

"Deinosuchus" means "terrible crocodile."

"Archelon" means "ancient turtle."

Glossary

ancient   from a very long time ago

cold-blooded   having a body temperature that is the same temperature as the surrounding air or water

fossil   something left behind by a plant or animal that has been preserved in the earth; examples are dinosaur bones and footprints.

jellyfish   a sea animal that has tentacles and a body that is soft like jelly

predator   an animal that hunts other animals for food

prey   an animal that is hunted by other animals for food

scales   small pieces of hard skin that cover the body of a reptile

shellfish   sea animals that live inside shells

swamp   an area of wet, spongy land

wingspan   the distance between the outer tips of an animal's wings

Index